REMEMBRANCE DAY

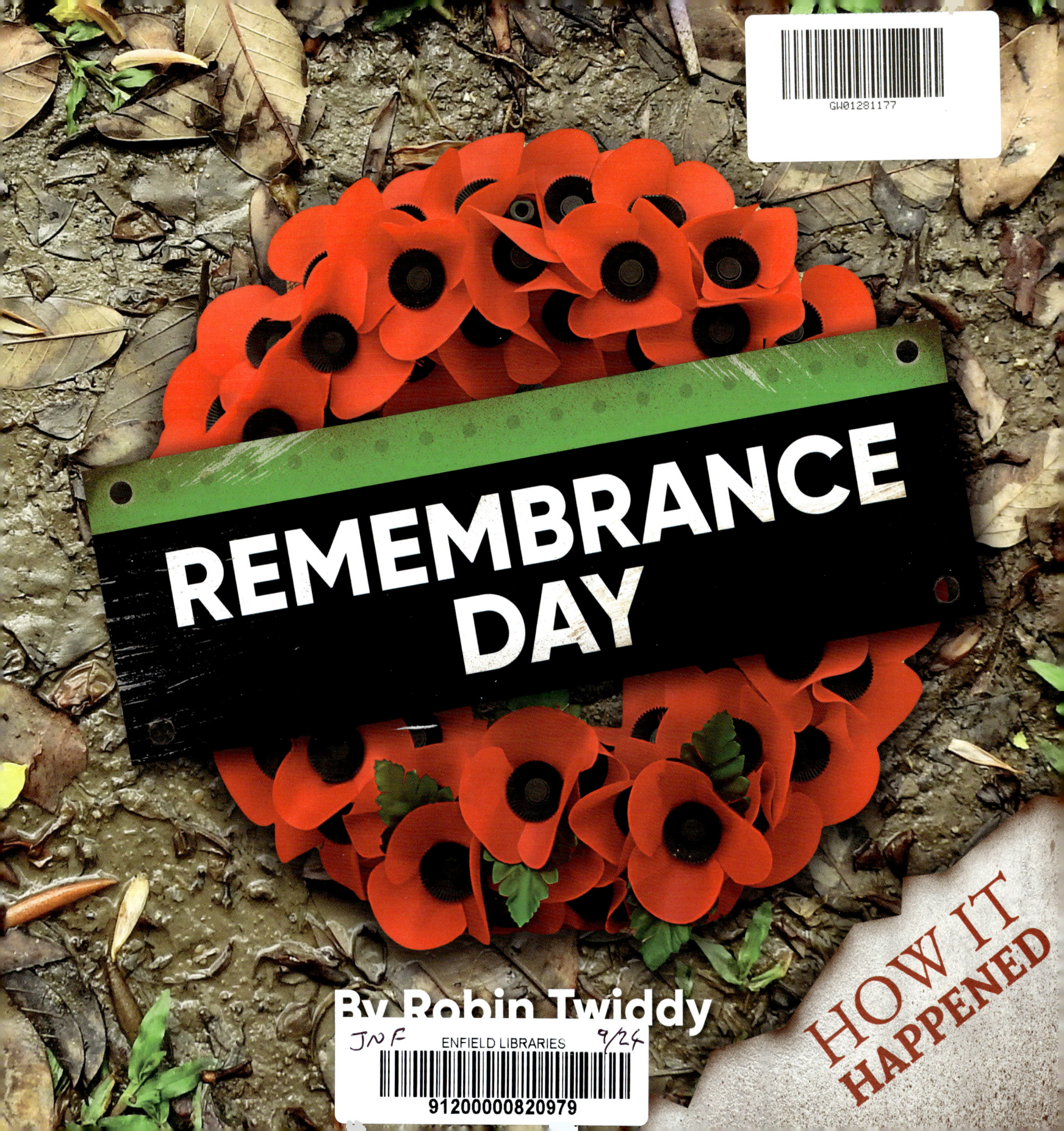

By Robin Twiddy

HOW IT HAPPENED

Written by:
Robin Twiddy

Edited by:
Madeline Tyler

Designed by:
Gareth Liddington

©This edition published 2024.
First published in 2022.
BookLife Publishing Ltd.
King's Lynn, Norfolk,
PE30 4LS, UK

HB ISBN: 978-1-83927-447-3
PB ISBN: 978-1-80505-672-0

A catalogue record for this book is available from the British Library.

All rights reserved. Printed in India.

All facts, statistics, web addresses and URLs in this book were verified as valid and accurate at time of writing. No responsibility for any changes to external websites or references can be accepted by either the author or publisher.

London Borough of Enfield	
91200000820979	
Askews & Holts	19-Sep-2024
J940.46 JUNIOR NON-F	
ENWINC	

Photo credits:

Front Cover – Willequet Manuel, Ken stocker, PHILIPIMAGE, 2&3 – Mariyana Lozanova, 4&5 – Everett Collection, Bikeworldtravel, design36, 6&7 – Monkey Business Images, Rido, Vladvm, 8&9 – Ed Samuel Theo Moonoi, Everett Collection, 12&13 – Everett Collection, FabrikaSimf, Pimbrils, Kilic inan, Gavran333, Mike Pellini, 14&15 – wavebreakmedia, Everett Collection, 16&17 – Andrew Harker, Franco aq, Andre Kritzinger, Gary Blakeley, Seregam, Everett Collection, 18&19 – Macrovector, 20&21 – ESB Professional, Milleflore Images, Leigh Prather, Everett Collection, 22&23 – Elena Lapshina.

Images are courtesy of Shutterstock.com. With thanks to Getty Images, Thinkstock Photo and iStockphoto.

CONTENTS

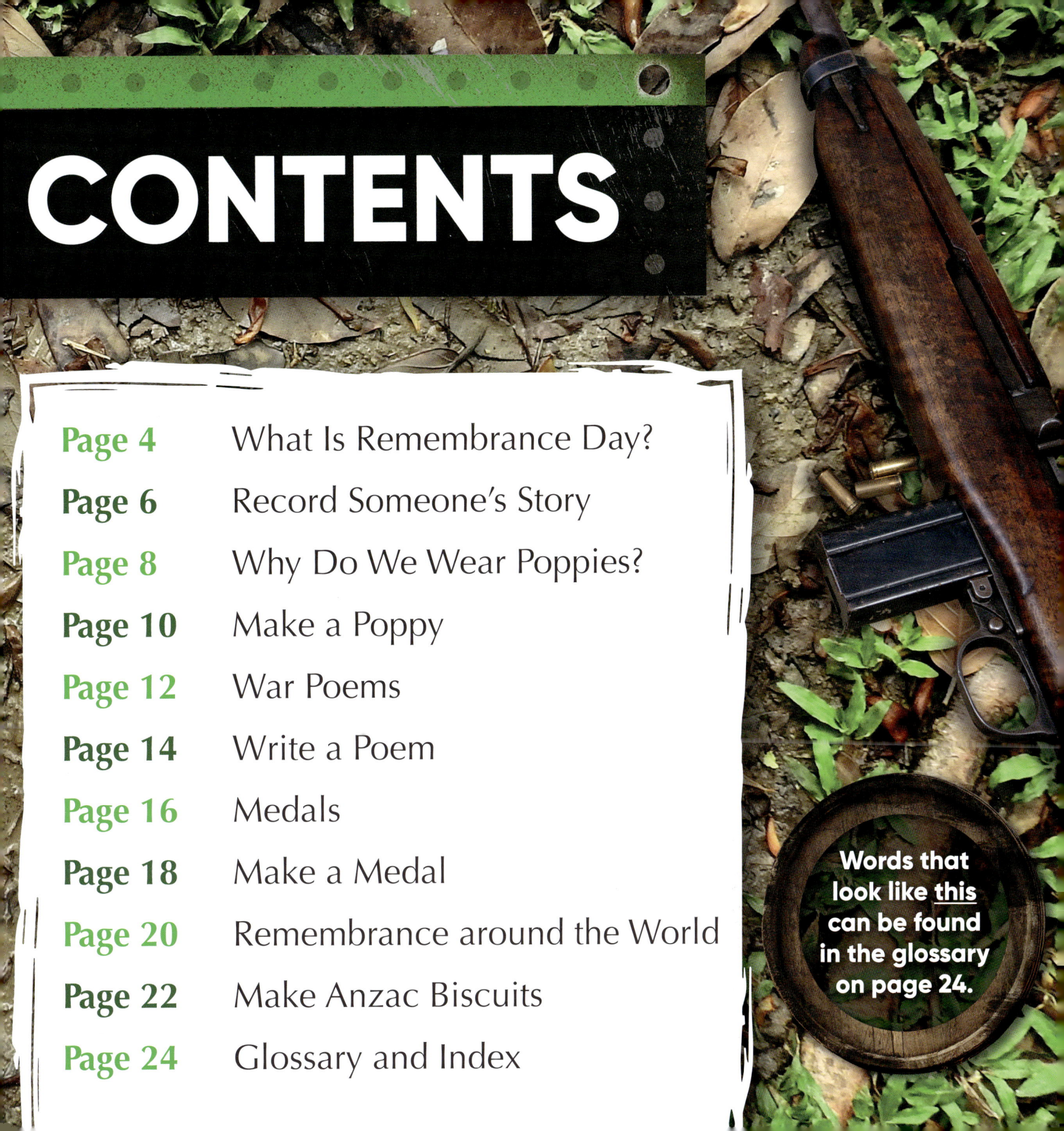

Page 4 — What Is Remembrance Day?

Page 6 — Record Someone's Story

Page 8 — Why Do We Wear Poppies?

Page 10 — Make a Poppy

Page 12 — War Poems

Page 14 — Write a Poem

Page 16 — Medals

Page 18 — Make a Medal

Page 20 — Remembrance around the World

Page 22 — Make Anzac Biscuits

Page 24 — Glossary and Index

Words that look like <u>this</u> can be found in the glossary on page 24.

WHAT IS REMEMBRANCE DAY?

Each year on the 11th of November, people <u>observe</u> Armistice Day, also known as Remembrance Day. It marks the day World War One ended.

28th July 1914
World War One begins

4

On Remembrance Day, we remember all the people who were lost in wars, not just in World War One.

Some of the wars that are remembered are:
World War One
World War Two
The Vietnam War
The Falklands War
Afghanistan War
Iraq War

World War One ended at 11 in the morning on the 11th day of the 11th month in 1918.

RECORD SOMEONE'S STORY

History is the things that have happened. Recording history can help us remember things. Recording something means writing it down. See if you can find someone in your family who can tell you about when they were young.

Important Things to Record

- Make sure to get any dates right.

- Are any other people mentioned in the memory? Make sure to get their names.

- Do they talk about how they felt in the memory?

WHY DO WE WEAR POPPIES?

You may notice that people pin poppies to their clothes or put up pictures of poppies around Remembrance Day. This is because the poppy has become a <u>symbol</u> for remembering soldiers lost at war.

28th July 1914
World War One begins

11th November 1918
World War One ends

After World War One ended, the <u>battlefields</u> filled with red poppies. Because of this, they became a symbol for soldiers who lost their lives in the war.

STEP 1
Flatten and paint your cake case red. Leave to dry.

STEP 2
Draw a black circle in the middle of your red cake case.

STEP 3
Cut a leaf shape out of green card.

STEP 4
Glue the leaf to the back of the poppy.

STEP 5
Glue the stick or pipe cleaner to the back of the poppy to make the stem.

Now your poppy is finished!

WAR POEMS

There are lots of ways to remember history. One way is through poetry. Lots of poets fought in World War One and wrote about it on the battlefields or when they came home.

28th July 1914 World War One begins

11th November 1918 World War One ends

11th November 1919 The first Remembrance Day

In the Trenches

I snatched two poppies
From the parapet's edge,
Two bright red poppies
That winked on the ledge.
Behind my ear
I stuck one through,
One blood red poppy
I gave to you.

A poem by Isaac Rosenberg

Isaac Rosenberg

How does the poem make you feel? Talk about it with your teacher or your friends.

WRITE A POEM

People write poems to explain a feeling or an idea. Poems can rhyme, but they don't have to. They can be long or short.

See if you can write a poem about something important to you.

Choose a word and write it down the side of the page. Now use each letter to start a line in your poem like this:

People make poems to show how they feel,
One word leads on to the next.
Every word as important as the last,
Making poetry is the best!

MEDALS

Soldiers are given medals when they are brave or do something that needs to be remembered. Sometimes medals are sent to the families of soldiers who don't come back from war.

28th July 1914
World War One begins

11th November 1918
World War One ends

11th November 1919
The first Remembrance Day

The 1914–15 Star

The British War Medal

The Victoria Cross

The 1914–15 Star, the British War Medal and the Victory Medal were known as Pip, Squeak and Wilfred.

The Victory Medal

These are some medals that have been given out:

1st September 1939
World War Two begins

STEP 1
Cut a piece of cardboard into the shape you want for your medal. Stars are good for medals.

STEP 2
Wrap it in foil, being careful not to get bumps or wrinkles.

STEP 3
Glue your ribbon to the back of the medal.

STEP 4
Stick to someone's jumper with sticky tape.

Get an adult to help with the cutting.

Now find someone who deserves a medal to stick it on.

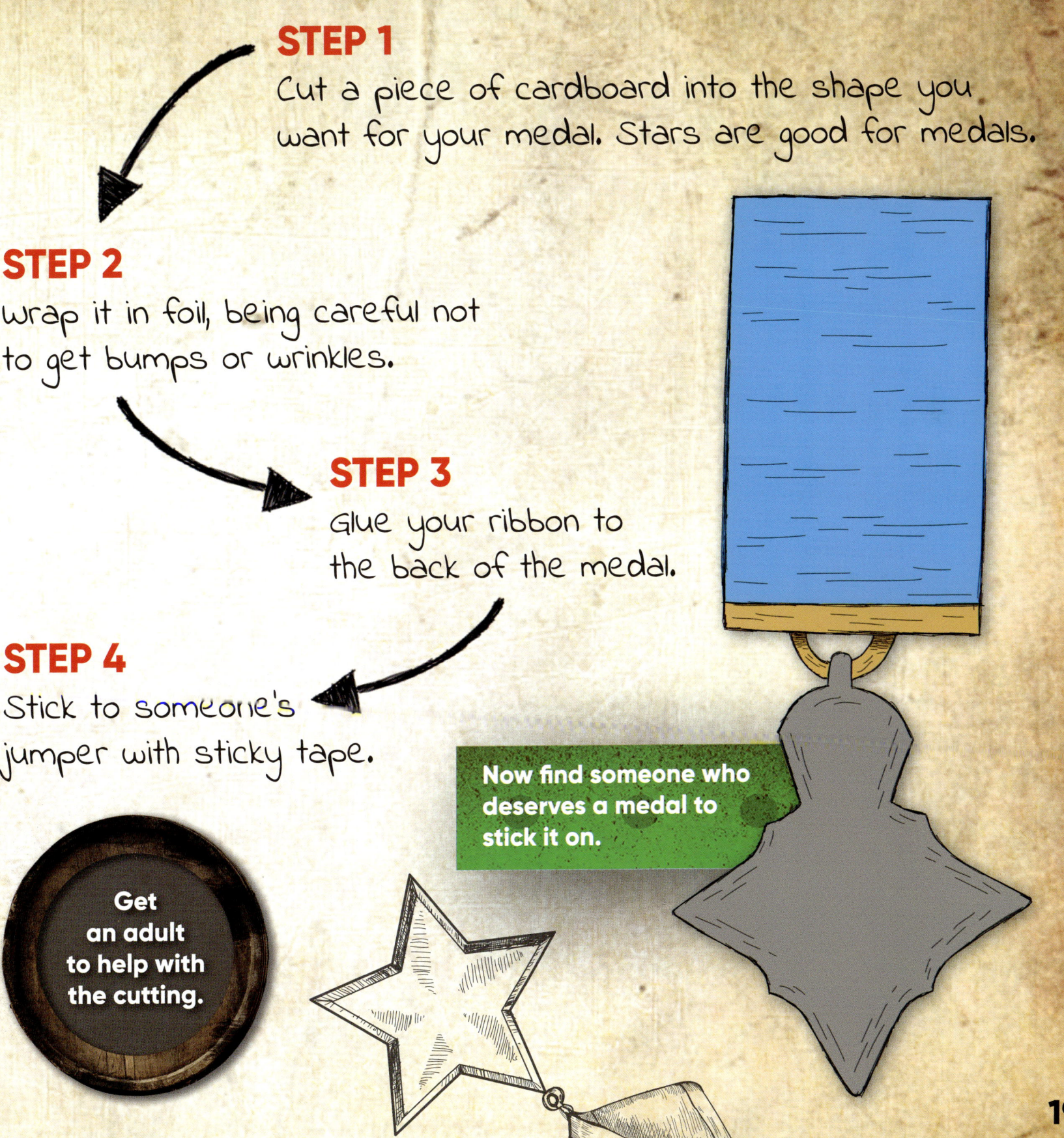

REMEMBRANCE AROUND THE WORLD

Some countries have something similar to Remembrance Day or mark it on a different day. The US has Veterans Day and Memorial Day. These are important days for remembering.

Veterans Day is on the 11th of November and is for remembering people who have served in the <u>military</u>.

28th July 1914
World War One begins

11th November 1918
World War One ends

11th November 1919
The first Remembrance Day

Anzac Day is on the 25th of April each year.

Australia and New Zealand remember lost soldiers and other military <u>personnel</u> on Anzac Day. Children make and sell Anzac biscuits to raise money.

1st September 1939
World War Two begins

2nd September 1945
World War Two ends

21

MAKE ANZAC BISCUITS

You will need:

- 150 grams of sugar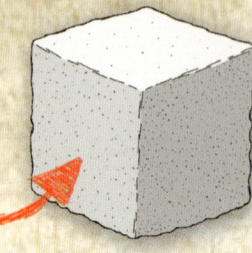
- 90 grams of golden syrup 
- 150 grams of unsalted butter
- Half a teaspoon of bicarbonate of soda 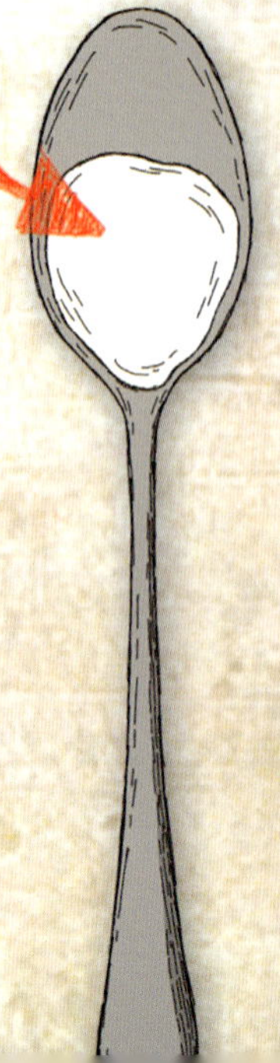
- 150 grams of plain flour
- 110 grams of coconut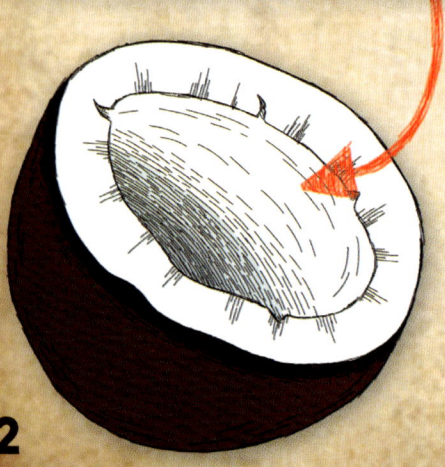
- 110 grams of rolled oats 
- 1 tablespoon of water

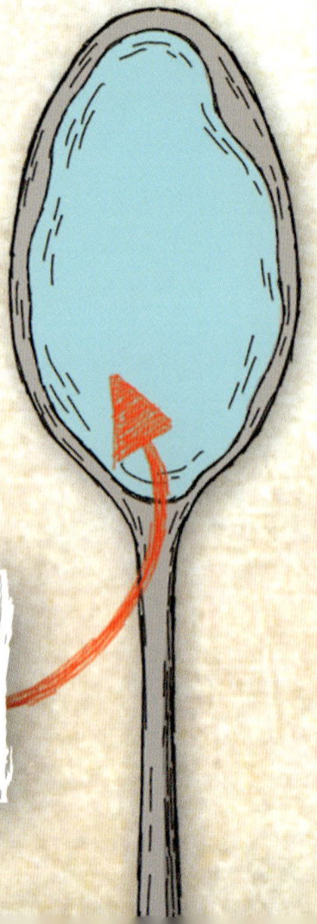

22

STEP 1
Preheat your oven to 175 degrees Celsius.

STEP 2
Mix the oats, flour, sugar and coconut together.

STEP 3
Melt the butter in a saucepan, then add golden syrup, water and bicarbonate of soda.

STEP 4
Mix the liquid into the dry ingredients.

STEP 5
Drop teaspoons of the mix onto greased baking paper.

STEP 6
Bake for 18 to 20 minutes.

GLOSSARY

battlefields	the places where fighting happens
military	to do with war, warfare and preparing for war
observe	pay attention to
parapet	a wall of earth or stone made to protect soldiers from the people they are fighting
personnel	all of the people who work for a business or group
symbol	something that stands for something else

INDEX

Australia 21
biscuits 21–23
bravery 16, 18
memory 7
poetry 12–15

poppies 8–11, 13
soldiers 8–9, 16, 21
trenches 13
US, the 20

World War One 4–5, 8–9, 12, 16, 20
World War Two 5, 17, 21